THE POWER STYLE

HOW FASHION AND BEAUTY ARE BEING USED TO RECLAIM CULTURES

CHRISTIAN ALLAIRE

annick press
toronto • berkeley

Front cover photograph of Neshay Linton photographed by Cameron Linton, provided courtesy of Jamie Okuma
Back cover photographs (from left to right) provided courtesy of Haute Hijab/Caleb & Gladys, Syro, and Tranquil Ashes/Cookie Monsta

Page 90 constitutes an extension of this copyright page.

Cover design by Paul Covello and Maegan Fidelino
Interior design by Maegan Fidelino
Edited by Mary Beth Leatherdale
Copyedit by Doeun Rivendell
Proofread by Mary Ann Blair
Expert read by Kelly Boutsalis

Annick Press Ltd.

We acknowledge the support of the Canada Council for the Arts and the Ontario Arts Council, and the participation of the Government of Canada/la participation du gouvernement du Canada for our publishing activities.

ONTARIO ARTS COUNCIL
CONSEIL DES ARTS DE L'ONTARIO
an Ontario government agency
un organisme du gouvernement de l'Ontario

Library and Archives Canada Cataloguing in Publication

Title: The power of style : how fashion and beauty are being used to reclaim cultures / Christian Allaire.
Names: Allaire, Christian, 1992- author.
Identifiers: Canadiana (print) 20200328859 | Canadiana (ebook) 20200328883 | ISBN 9781773214900 (hardcover) | ISBN 9781773214917 (softcover) | ISBN 9781773214924 (HTML) | ISBN 9781773214931 (PDF) | ISBN 9781773214948 (Kindle)
Subjects: LCSH: Fashion—Juvenile literature. | LCSH: Fashion—Social aspects—Juvenile literature.
Classification: LCC GT518 .A45 2021 | DDC j391—dc23

Published in the U.S.A. by Annick Press (U.S.) Ltd.
Distributed in Canada by University of Toronto Press.
Distributed in the U.S.A. by Publishers Group West.

Printed in China

annickpress.com
christianjallaire.com
jacqln-li.com

Also available as an e-book. Please visit annickpress.com/ebooks for more details.

To all the kids who feel like they aren't seen or heard,
this book is dedicated to you.

—C.A.

CONTENTS

INTRODUCTION

Aanin, hello.

This book is for anyone who has never felt represented, who has felt inferior or less beautiful, and who has questioned their roots.

My journey toward writing this book began back in 2014, when I was studying fashion journalism in Toronto. I decided that I would focus on writing about fashion through a more inclusive lens, something I now do as a fashion and style writer for *Vogue* magazine.

Along the way, I began meeting people like me—other writers, designers, and artists from a variety of cultures, all of whom felt a lack of representation in the fashion and beauty industries. I am Ojibwe and grew up loving fashion, but I rarely saw my people represented in magazines or in movies. Navigating my own experiences, and meeting those who shared them, led me to write this very book.

Fashion holds more power than you think. Its role as something more than just *pretty clothes and bags and shoes* has been debated for a long time. In fact, fashion wasn't even considered serious art until recent exhibits devoted to fashion started popping up at major museums (such as the Met's Costume Institute, for instance). It does raise the question: Can fashion or beauty serve a greater purpose than just being visually satisfying? Can a fashion designer or model or entrepreneur have a direct impact on how we feel about ourselves and those around us? The short answer is yes! And you're about to meet those who do.

The people you will meet in this book are using fashion and beauty to promote cultural activism, empowerment, diversity, and inclusivity. They are essentially using garments, accessories, or various beauty techniques to reclaim their identities and celebrate who they are. It is so important to recognize that our own cultures and upbringings are beautiful—and equally as important to learn about other cultures, too. These creatives show why style is such a great medium to explore this through; it delves into our unique communities and traditions in a striking—and dare I say, *fun and fabulous*—way.

This book will hopefully allow you to see how all things style-related can make us feel more *like us* at the end of the day. Enhance who we already are and help share our stories with others. And while these individuals, and their distinctive style choices, serve as a snapshot into North America's diverse population and beyond, they are certainly not all-encompassing. There's so much more out there to discover.
— Christian Allaire

SEWING TRADITION

Through making (and wearing!) ribbon work, the Indigenous community is keeping their culture's unique traditions alive.

WHAT IS RIBBON WORK?

Ribbon work is a traditional design craft, popular in many Indigenous tribes, in which colorful ribbons are applied onto shirts, dresses, and skirts. The colors of the ribbons, and how they are applied, typically have personal significance to the wearer.

MY CULTURE'S COUTURE

Through having his very own ribbon shirt made, **Christian Allaire** discovered that Indigenous design is about more than creating a garment. It's about maintaining traditional craft and honoring your family roots.

Christian Allaire, the author of this book.

FAMILY TIES

Growing up, I was always obsessed with all things fashion. Yet I rarely saw myself represented in this industry. I am Indigenous (Ojibwe) and grew up on the Nipissing First Nation reservation, where I was constantly surrounded by beauty—the stunning regalia worn at powwows being a prime example. But when I looked at the pages of a magazine or the big screen, I rarely saw anyone who looked like the people I grew up with. This caused a certain sense of shame in my youth; I always felt inferior to the peers who I felt were more represented in mainstream pop culture.

FINDING PRIDE

It took me a long time to realize that, no, I actually am proud of who I am. Nowadays, I have a growing appreciation for traditional Indigenous design. It is often rooted in something much deeper. Traditional garments are embedded with special meaning: whether it's Ojibwe, Cree, Lakota—each tribe holds unique craftwork that has been passed down through the generations. When you see traditional regalia worn at a powwow, the wearers aren't sporting them just for the pretty aesthetic (though, yes, they are pretty)—they're wearing these garments as a way to keep their culture alive and to honor their ancestors by bringing the specialties they've perfected over generations into the present day. A prime example of cultural fashion in my tribe is ribbon work, and by having my first adult ribbon shirt made, I developed a closer connection to my heritage in the process.

My ribbon shirt team: from left, my auntie Tammy; my mother, Nancy; my auntie Joan; and my auntie Lee.

THE PAST AND PRESENT OF RIBBON WORK

HISTORY OF THE RIBBON SHIRT

Indigenous ribbon work became popular in the 18th century. French traders brought silk over from Europe to the Great Lakes region of North America. At that time, fanciful ribbons were falling out of fashion with Europeans, yet decorative ribbons began thriving in the designs of Indigenous people, who began experimenting with the new materials and putting their own unique cultural twists on them.

CONSULTING MY ELDERS

I come from a large family of Indigenous garment makers—my mom is one of 18 siblings, and many of my aunties are extremely talented with a sewing machine—so I decided it was finally time to have my own adult ribbon shirt made. My late grandmother, Leda, made me a ribbon shirt when I was child, and my new one is modeled after it as a special way to acknowledge her spirit. My first step was asking my elders—my mother, father, and living grandparents—what their favorite colors are. Their choices are reflected in the colors of the ribbons sewed onto my shirt as a way to acknowledge my roots and where I come from. After consulting them, I landed on these colors: red, blue, yellow, white, black, and gray. Some of these hues are also represented in the four colors of our medicine wheel teachings; in Ojibwe culture, the medicine wheel represents the four directions and the four elements of the earth (earth, wind, water, and fire). Having these four colors on my shirt represents living a life that is balanced.

THE RIBBON SHIRT TODAY

These days, ribbon work workshops are used in Indigenous communities as a way to inspire creativity, bond the people within the gathering, and carry on their specific tribe's design traditions. The workshops are usually led by an elder who can guide newcomers on creating their own designs. The ribbon work can be applied onto a variety of pieces: men's shirts, women's dresses, and skirts. Ribbons are also often incorporated in traditional regalia, such as jingle dresses, and are worn by dancers at powwow ceremonies.

HONORING FAMILY DESIGN

After deciding on the ribbon colors, I chose a style of ribbon work to be sewed onto the shirt. I decided on a navy blue shirt as my base—a color I feel most comfortable in—and then for the ribbons to be sewn on top as horizontal accents across the chest and around the cuffs; it's a style of ribbon work that my Ojibwe family has traditionally specialized in, and I decided to follow this aesthetic. The assembling didn't take long. My mother, Nancy, and my aunts Joan, Tammy, and Lee teamed up and got it done over a few weekends; first they took my custom measurements, and then sewed it together at my mother's house. Abalone shells were used to make the buttons.

On the back, a family friend, Tracey Larochelle, also embroidered an image of a crane to represent my clan.

WEARING IT WITH PRIDE

When I first slipped on my brand-new ribbon shirt, I couldn't wait to wear it to many upcoming cultural events. It is a symbolic way of using fashion as a means to pay homage to my roots. Now, whenever I wear it, I will not only feel a sense of pride tied to my culture, but I will also know that each ribbon represents those who are close to me and the physical love they put into this garment. It's more than just a shirt—it's a family heirloom.

WINNING RIBBONS

Indigenous fashion artists like **Jamie Okuma** are making use of ribbon work in new, unexpected ways. By combining tradition with innovation, they are helping drive the craft forward.

"When I look at traditional dresses and skirts, more often the ribbon is only on the skirt or lines the sleeves of wing dresses, but I like to cover the entire garment with ribbon. I've also made entire ensembles, with modern silhouettes, completely out of silk ribbon." — Jamie Okuma

Jamie Okuma is an Indigenous (Luiseño and Shoshone-Bannock) fashion artist based in the La Jolla Indian Reservation in Pauma Valley, California.

SPIRITUAL CONNECTIONS

Anita Fields's work—which is on display in many museums and galleries—respects her Indigenous culture's traditional way of doing ribbon work. Unlike those of more contemporary designers, many of her pieces are specifically made for cultural ceremonies.

Wedding coat

Anita Fields is an Osage and Muscogee (Creek) artist based in Tulsa, Oklahoma.

KEEPING HISTORY ALIVE

"Osage work uses vivid, brilliant colors. Our patterns are predominantly geometric. We are still using the patterns you see in historic photos—the double arrow, diamonds, and the double heart design are a few to name. In the beginning we used cotton strips; as our skills and knowledge grew, we started creating with satin and taffeta ribbons."

THINKING POSITIVE

"Making ribbon work is an act of the heart. It is so much more than simply picking up a needle and thread. Your process would begin with a prayer and good thoughts for the wearer. Your good thoughts would include the importance of the garment and its importance to our culture."

HONORING CEREMONY

"When a male takes on the role of drumkeeper for our In'Lonshka ceremonial dance, there is a ceremony where the drumkeeper's family dresses several female relatives in Osage clothes and wedding coats. This is known as paying for the drum; it is sharing gifts as a way to acknowledge the honor of being selected as drumkeeper. I've made ribbon work skirts for two relatives. Becoming a drumkeeper is a big commitment, and families have a year to prepare for this ceremony, so relatives offer their help to put the clothing together."

ANITA'S STEP-BY-STEP GUIDE TO RIBBON WORK

"Osage ribbon work has several techniques. I learned to baste down all work before sewing on a machine, but many of the old works are totally done with tiny, intricate stitches."

1. Sew two strips of ribbon together as a base.

2. Baste a ribbon into place on top of each ribbon on the base. Now you have a double-sided strip of ribbons.

3. Place the pattern on top of each ribbon and draw on the design.

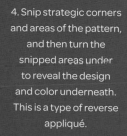

4. Snip strategic corners and areas of the pattern, and then turn the snipped areas under to reveal the design and color underneath. This is a type of reverse appliqué.

Anita made this wedding skirt for her daughter.

PAVING THE WAY

Crow and Northern Cheyenne designer **Bethany Yellowtail**
was raised on the Crow Indian Reservation in southern Montana.
It was on her traditional territory that she was first exposed to
ribbon work, which continues to serve as a motif in her fashion designs.

REINVENTING THE PAST

"My earliest memories are seeing ribbon work on fancy
dance shawls at the Crow Fair, our tribe's largest powwow," Yellowtail says. "I especially loved seeing ribbon
work at the traditional Handgames tournaments, where
ribbons and appliqué are used to adorn each district
member competing."

While her fashions are more on the contemporary
side, Yellowtail pays homage to her culture's vibrant
aesthetic in her own unique way: "I have used ribbon
work very minimally in my designs," she says. "My
favorite piece is a vintage-inspired sweetheart dress
with fabric that reminds me of my *kaale* (grandmother).
I used four rows of brightly colored twill ribbon as a nod
to traditional ribbon skirts."

Her work is trailblazing in that it encourages fellow
Indigenous designers to take approaches to their
culture that are not the norm—albeit in a way that is still
respectful to traditions. "Respectfully utilizing traditional ways of creating, like ribbon work techniques, is
an opportunity to culture share and create bridges of
understanding, while also positively impacting Native
peoples," she says. "There is nothing better than getting
messages from Native women and allies who tell me
they feel beautiful, powerful, and protected when they
wear my work out into the world."

> "Ribbon work is a true testament to the resourcefulness of our communities. It's beautiful to see what can be done with minimal supplies to create striking, bold garments." — Bethany Yellowtail

CULTURAL APPROPRIATION VS. APPRECIATION

CULTURAL APPROPRIATION

Cultural appropriation occurs when members of one culture adopt elements of another culture without their consent. This happens often in the fashion world: Indigenous design motifs have been long copied or replicated by non-Indigenous fashion brands, who often misuse traditional elements or ignore a piece's original purpose.

CULTURAL APPRECIATION

There is a right way to be inspired or pay homage to another culture, however. By buying pieces from authentic artists (such as Bethany Yellowtail, Jamie Okuma, and others mentioned in this chapter), you are supporting a community by going straight to the source. Non-Indigenous brands can also collaborate with Indigenous artists by involving them in the design process to guarantee a more accurate end result.

#TRENDING

Ribbon work is exploding in popularity. Indigenous designers are approaching it in both traditional and offbeat ways. As a result, more wearers are rocking the designs in their own special ways, too.

MY HAIR, MY WAY

Our hair can represent our individuality, but many of us have deep-rooted relationships with it that go beyond just a preferred style. From learning to love our natural textures to the cultural reasons some keep it long, how we wear our hair can have a much deeper meaning.

WHAT IS NATURAL HAIR?

Natural hair is exactly what it
sounds like: hair that is natural. In the Black community,
wearing one's hair naturally is
a power move. It counters the
years of being told that their
hair is inferior or "less beautiful" than white people's. While
many have gladly shed their
harsh, and often damaging,
hair treatments in the quest
for perfect, pin-straight locks,
the journey to self-acceptance
hasn't always been easy.

LOVE THY LOCKS

Modupe Oloruntoba is a writer and editor based in Johannesburg, South Africa. Growing up, she relaxed her hair and felt going natural wasn't an option. In her own words, she shares her long journey toward learning to accept, and even love, her natural locks and explains why the pressure to get pin-straight hair is a common struggle for many other Black women, too.

EARLY MEMORIES

"I don't remember a time when my hair wasn't relaxed [to get rid of the natural curl]. I kicked up a major fuss whenever it was time to get it done. When I was 11 or 12, my mother made the big chop she had threatened for years if doing my hair continued to be a loud struggle. We were at her friend's barbershop and the razor came out. I remember crying, not because I was natural now, but because I thought I looked like a boy. I was natural for a while after that. My hair would grow out, and when it was long enough to look good straight, I would relax it again. It was obvious, the unspoken expectation."

DEALING WITH MAINTENANCE

"Hair care is enjoyable for some people. It has never been that for me. I desperately wanted, and still want, taking care of my hair to be as clinical and straightforward as buttoning a shirt or brushing my teeth. Relaxed or natural, I wasn't interested in spending hours on it for any reason. I remember wishing my hair would just do itself. I decided to transition to natural hair in 2015 out of curiosity. When I made that transition, I had to do it myself.

"Americans have this idea that Africans in Africa have always known what to do with our hair and had technique and product down, but for the most part we haven't—not me, and not any girl I knew. We were learning from scratch and without much help. Some sort of hair struggle story is common among Black men and women. In the past, the fashion and beauty industries have promoted key characteristics of natural hair as undesirable. Part of the problem is how brands and media focus only on what we have in common. My experience of my natural hair is different from both my sisters', and we all grew up in the same house."

MY LOVE-HATE RELATIONSHIP WITH HAIR CARE

"Learning about natural hair made me feel like I had to become an expert in care and styling overnight, just to leave the house with nice-looking hair and not feel like I was damaging it. That felt unfair. It felt even worse when I saw how some Black women responded to what I felt was extra work: these women were proud of the work. So much so that certain corners of the natural-hair conversation began to feel like the content only existed to show you how much more work some women put into their hair than others. Yes, a lot of us don't relax our hair anymore, but so many of us replaced the focus on bone straight hair with an obsession with endless mousses and gels to banish frizz and lay down edges, and the industry responded with products to fuel the pursuit of that new ideal. We deserve the option of simplicity."

"We're not quite neutral yet, my fro and me, but I obviously know much more about myself now than I did as a child."
— Modupe Oloruntoba

WHAT IS RELAXED HAIR?

Relaxed hair involves using a chemical lotion or cream to straighten its natural texture. To avoid breakage, protein or moisturizing treatments are often encouraged with it. The procedure usually lasts around eight weeks before a touch-up is needed.

OVER THE RAINBOW

With the quick change of a hairstyle—from the color to the length—drag queens can bring new characters and personas to life on stage. By rocking fabulous hair, however, queens also unleash their innate creativity—their exterior glam matches their interior beauty. Here, Vancouver-based Cree queen **Quanah Style** breaks down the importance of a dramatic hair look.

"Wigs help me feel the fantasy and complete the looks! I probably have around 30 wigs now. I prefer wigs with soft lace fronts, and custom pieces are fab for special events or shoots." — Quanah Style

AT ANY LENGTH

Chelene Knight is the President of Breathing Space Creative Literary Studio. As a professional creative, Knight has noticed that how she wears her hair can greatly influence how people perceive her.

WHAT WAS YOUR EXPERIENCE WITH NATURAL HAIR GROWING UP?

"When I was younger, I was confused. I was constantly told that I had good hair but had no idea what that meant. Growing up in a Black family and being mixed-race (my father is East Indian), I was often singled out as being the ideal in terms of my hair. In other situations and circumstances outside of family, I was seen as (and I hate to use this word) exotic. That always bothered me. I always dreamed of straight hair, the kind of you didn't have to 'worry about'—the kind that stayed straight while swimming, in the rain, and with even the slightest hint of moisture in the air."

HOW HAVE PEOPLE INTERACTED WITH YOUR NATURAL HAIR?

"Within the constructs of my family, my hair was not considered inferior; it was considered ideal. But in terms of the way my hair was looked at outside of my family, it was different. As an adult, it affects me a lot less than it did 20 years ago, but I often feel 'less than' or not included when I am around Black women who do not identify as mixed. I am often told I don't 'look Black' and that adds a whole new layer of confusion and inferiority."

DOES HOW YOU WEAR YOUR HAIR CHANGE HOW PEOPLE PERCEIVE YOU?

"Yes. My hair in its natural state is just a big soft puff. Not an Afro-type puff but a puff that looks deflated at the crown and expands from the roots. This is not even a style, it's just . . . there. But if I add mousse when the hair is wet, I have an opportunity to have hair that will look luxurious and full in four to six hours (aka the drying time). Or, if I opt to braid my hair, then, well, because that is considered a 'Black style,' I receive no questions, and assumptions arrive."

IS IT A COMMON EXPERIENCE FOR BLACK PEOPLE TO HAVE A COMPLICATED RELATIONSHIP WITH THEIR HAIR?

"The Black hair industry is a business. Natural hair doesn't suit the growing business. So I mean, it's like getting a salad at Burger King: people are there for the burgers (straight hair), but you still have to offer 'healthy options,' and natural hair is that option. No one is catering to support Black women rocking natural hair. Why? Because there is no money in natural hair for businesses. But I like my hair as it grows out of my head and, to be honest, I have no energy to fight that."

NATURAL HAIR ON THE RED CARPET

Celebrities are bringing natural hairstyles to the red carpet and completely rocking them in the process, proving that embracing one's true self can be a style statement of its own.

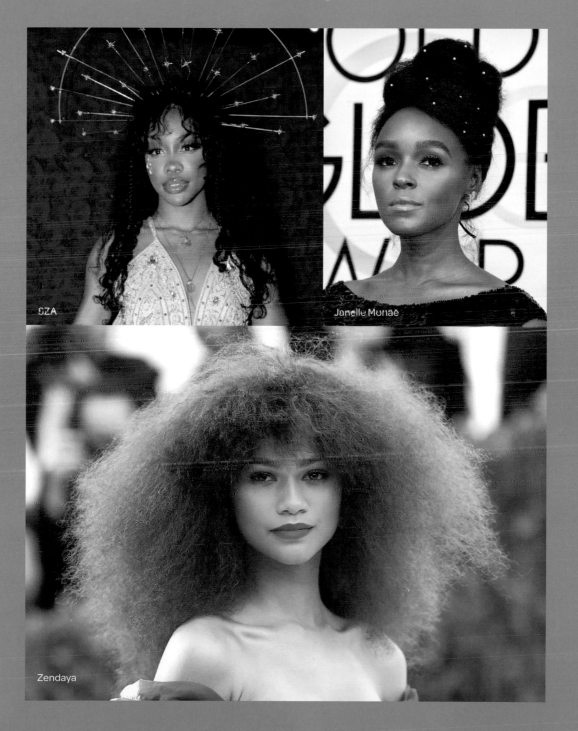

SZA

Janelle Monáe

Zendaya

GROWING FREEDOM

For Indigenous men, maintaining long hair is more than just a stylistic choice. It represents an upholding of cultural tradition and an unwillingness to conform.

Haatepah Clearbear is a model from the Kumeyaay, Pai Pai, and Chicimeca-Guamare nations.

"Long hair to me is a symbol of pride. A pride that has been marketed as shameful by Western belief systems. Back in the day, Indigenous children across the Americas were forced into boarding schools, and the idea was to kill the Indian, save the man. They cut off our hair and would physically and mentally abuse us to forget our cultural ways and language and to forcefully take on someone else's. I wear my hair long to honor my ancestors and the sacrifice they made, because they didn't have a choice. I have the option to grow it long. So I hold my hair with pride."
— Haatepah Clearbear

"From the day I was born until now, I've never had a haircut. Despite what you may think, my hair care isn't very complicated. Simply, it's shampoo, conditioner, and coconut oil. For most tribes on the Plains, it's tradition for us men to grow our hair long. It's our spirit. I wear my hair in two braids to keep that tradition going." — Phillip Bread

Phillip Bread is a model from the Comanche, Kiowa, and Blackfeet nations.

James Jones is a Cree dancer and performer.

"My ancestors had long hair, and there was a time when many of my people were forced to cut their hair in residential schools. The government tried to take away our culture and assimilate us to look and act like them. I wear my hair long and proud to honor my ancestors and teach the younger generation to be proud of who they are." — James Jones

THE ART OF BRAIDS

A longtime wearer of braids and other natural styles, **Durrant Santeng** collaborated with two hair artists for a one-of-a-kind look.

Durrant Santeng is a senior designer for *Vogue* magazine.

CREATIVE COLLABORATION

"In the midst of one of my usual hair-braiding appointments with Guingui Pérez, she came across the old Windows logo and presented it to me and Ivan Nova (my go-to master barber). Spontaneously, she proposed the idea of recreating the design as a pattern with my hair. Nova and I were immediately interested. To document this experiment, Nova recruited his girlfriend, photographer Nalin Springer, to capture this collaboration, pictured here."

SWITCHING IT UP

"I try a new hairstyle every year. Over the years I've had waves, Afros, a high-top fade, my natural curls with an undercut, and, recently, braids of different styles. My mother was working as a hairdresser when she had me. I was born with an unusual amount of hair, so we had a lot to play with. I wore buns and braids, and I had the occasional haircut when it grew too long. My brother and I spent our early years with our grandparents in Accra, Ghana, where I experimented with my hair. During this time, I even gave Jheri curls and perms a shot!"

BRAID STYLES

From sleek box braids to more statement-making crochet braids, our personal style can be reflected in the way we wear our hair. Here are five styles to know!

CORNROWS

BOX BRAIDS

CROCHET BRAIDS

BRAIDED BANTU KNOTS

FAUX LOCS

LEVEL-UP

Today's cosplayers are disrupting the art form, promoting
self-confidence, acceptance, and body positivity along the way.

Cosplayer Surely Shirley in action.

WHAT IS COSPLAY?

Cosplay—combining the words *costume* and *play*—is the art of dressing up like a fictional character. The character can be from a variety of mediums including anime, comic books, classic literature, TV shows, movies, video games, and more—as long as the character has a distinguishable look. Typically, cosplayers try to dress up as close as possible to the original character, though there are some cosplayers who prefer to put their own original twist on it, infusing their own identity and flair into their outfits.

WHY WE COSPLAY

Cosplayers create costumes that are skillfully made and totally unique. In the process of making their art, they also promote positive relationships with both themselves and others.

Kaptain76, aka Kap, is a cosplayer based in Southern California.

"**Cosplaying feels like a transformation. Sometimes, when in a character, it's not just about being dressed up as the character—it's *becoming* that character. Their attitude becomes your own, and it can feel even more freeing than just dressing as them.**" — Kaptain76

"Cosplay has absolutely increased my confidence level. It shows that you can be whoever you want to be. Besides, who wouldn't want to be their own superhero?" — Anita Riggs

Anita Riggs, aka Tranquil Ashes, is a cosplayer based in Baltimore, Maryland.

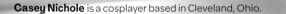

Casey Nichole is a cosplayer based in Cleveland, Ohio.

"Cosplay allows me to be creative and challenges me to try new things. As a plus-size cosplayer, I try to show others that they can cosplay whoever they want to be. My size does not stop me from cosplaying my favorite characters." — Casey Nichole

> "I have definitely found like-minded cosplayers, and we will continue to make sure that cosplay really truly is for everyone. We can make that difference." — Shirley Melendez

Shirley Melendez, aka Surely Shirley, is a cosplayer based in Palm Beach, Florida.

MY BODY, MY CHOICE

The cosplay community can be strict when it comes to rules: guidelines suggest that cosplayers must have the same body type as the characters they are portraying. But new players are changing the rules by being who they want, when they want. And as a result of dressing up, they feel more comfortable in their own skin!

Kaptain76, aka Kap, is a plus-size cosplayer. Through her innovative costumes, she is challenging cosplay norms and making a statement: beauty isn't one-size-fits-all.

MAKING MY OWN RULES

"It can often be hard for plus-size cosplayers to get attention, despite putting in just as much work as, or even more than, a slimmer counterpart. The number of people-of-color characters is low, and characters with varying body types is even lower, so people who don't necessarily look similar to their character can be bullied for being inaccurate. Maybe with open conversation and a push for change, things could be better in the future.

"Cosplaying in itself doesn't really promote body positivity. [However,] I do feel a sense of confidence when I'm in cosplay. Going through all of the work to become the character makes it easier for me to feel proud. Putting in such an insane amount of effort, and then being able to look at yourself when it's all done, makes it easy to feel empowered."

THE HISTORY OF COSPLAY

The art of cosplay dates back to North America in the 1930s. A man named Forrest J. Ackerman attended a sci-fi convention dressed up in a futuristic outfit. While he was not dressed as a specific character—which is what cosplaying is all about nowadays—he chose to dress to the event's theme. Ackerman's costume idea eventually caught on, and attendees began dressing up more and more for conventions. Then competitions began popping up at conventions, too, awarding the best dressed with prizes.

In 1984, the official term, *cosplay*, was coined in Japan. It was Nobuyuki Takahashi, then the founder of an anime studio called Studio Hard, who introduced the terminology after attending the Worldcon event in Los Angeles. He felt the word *masquerade* did not correctly describe what he saw, which was guests dressing up as—and acting like—their favorite characters from big TV shows.

BREAKING THE STATUS QUO

Traditionally, the cosplay space has enforced a rigid set of guidelines that players must follow. But diversity and freedom are on the rise thanks to players who are embracing their own identity and infusing it into their costumes.

Shirley Melendez, aka Surely Shirley, is a plus-size Latinx cosplayer. Through finding a like-minded family of cosplayers, she is encouraging a community based on originality.

GETTING INTO COSPLAY

"I was taught how to sew at a young age by my seamstress mother, and then I taught myself how to create props to go with my costumes."

FINDING HER CREW

"In the beginning, it was hard finding photographers who really made you feel great and empowered being shot by them. I had my body cropped out in photos because the photographer didn't realize I loved my body and wasn't ashamed of it, even though they were. Being part of the Latinx community and the plus-size community, I have found so many friends who feed positively off of each other and really promote each other."

CHALLENGING THE NORM

"People see the mainstream cosplay community as white or Asian females who are very thin; however, if you just look right outside of that, you'll find tons of groups and communities that cater to people of color, plus-size cosplayers, people with disabilities, and the whole spectrum of sexuality. We may not be as 'mainstream,' but we are powerful, constantly speaking out, and creating panels to discuss topics that people can relate to."

THE EXPLOSION OF COMIC-CON

Today, Comic-Con is one of the biggest—and most internationally recognized—conventions for cosplayers to gather. Comic-Con began on March 21, 1970. Founder Shel Dorf and a group of teenage comic book fans held a one-day comic "minicon" in San Diego, California. The event turned out to be a big success, and the group decided to hold a second "minicon" later that summer, where over 300 fans turned out. In 1973, the official gathering was established as the "San Diego Comic-Con." In the present day, cosplayers from around the globe now travel to Comic-Con to display their new works and costumes. Consider it the Oscars of the cosplay world!

CROSSING BOUNDARIES

Another rule of cosplaying is that players must be the same gender as the character they are portraying. But new rule-breakers are dressing up as their favorite characters of the opposite sex and challenging stereotypical gender roles as a result.

Anita Riggs, aka Tranquil Ashes, is a cosplayer who dresses up as both male and female characters. Instead of choosing them by gender, she is drawn to playing roles entirely based on personality.

"I don't have one type of cosplay that I do. However, I often go for powerful characters—whether they be male, female, nonbinary, or alien. Instead of replicating an outfit or look to the letter, I often tweak it into my own style and tastes." — Anita Riggs

GENDER-BEND VS. CROSSPLAY

Cosplayers are redefining gender norms with these two styles of dress.

GENDER-BEND
A cosplayer changes the gender of a character to fit their own.

CROSSPLAY
A cosplayer dresses as a character whose gender is different than their own.

DIY IT!

The art of cosplay demands a crafty skill set.
The only rules? There are no rules!

TRIAL AND ERROR

Cosplayers can assume any identity they want with the help of the right tools and a whole lot of creativity. Take Casey Nichole, a cosplayer based in Cleveland, Ohio: she got her start in the art form by learning how to make costumes from the Internet.

"I created my first cosplay, Harley Quinn from *Suicide Squad*, with items from the thrift store and hot glue. After that, I was hooked and wanted to create more. I started cosplaying knowing nothing about sewing or prop making. With YouTube and trial and error, I began to develop more skills and began competing in cosplay competitions."
— Casey Nichole

COSPLAY TOOLS

Ready to DIY your own look? These are some of the tools you'll need for that first costume.

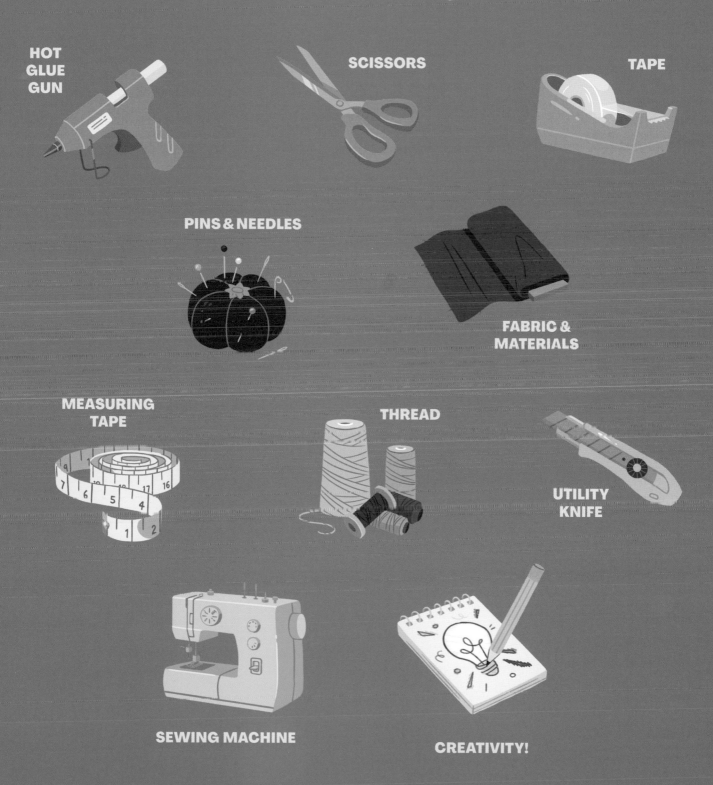

HOT GLUE GUN

SCISSORS

TAPE

PINS & NEEDLES

FABRIC & MATERIALS

MEASURING TAPE

THREAD

UTILITY KNIFE

SEWING MACHINE

CREATIVITY!

HEAD STRONG

Muslim women are embracing hijabs, but they're doing so on their own terms. They're celebrating their culture by embracing modest fashion in new, unexpected, and very stylish ways.

A look by Haute Hijab.

WHAT IS A HIJAB?

A hijab is a type of headscarf worn by Muslim women that covers both the head and neck but exposes the face. They come in an array of colors, prints, and fabrics.

WHAT IS MODEST FASHION?

Though it's not exclusive to one religion or group, many Muslim women choose to dress modestly. This includes covering up the body with pieces such as long pants, floor-length dresses, and sleeved tops, among other garments.

TAKING CONTROL

Melanie Elturk is reinventing the hijab by giving it a luxurious, on-trend twist. Here, the entrepreneur talks about how her stylish pieces are designed to offer Muslim women a new platform for self-expression while still respecting modest fashion guidelines.

"I've always loved wearing the hijab."
— Melanie Elturk

UNDERSTANDING THE HIJAB

"In the West, there's this misconception that Muslim women are forced into wearing the hijab. In certain parts of the world, that may be true; however, it's not true for the vast majority of Muslim women.

"There are also some people who believe that the only right way to wear a hijab is to wear a black hijab. We know that that is certainly not true; you dress according to the culture that you live in. If you live in Africa, Malaysia, or the United Kingdom, the way that you interpret those guidelines is going to be different. You see a lot more variety today in the ways women are expressing themselves."

MAKING IT MY OWN

"Not only do I wear the headscarf, I also dress modestly. Modest style is being able to decide how much of yourself you want to show to the world. It's really about not feeling like you have to dress a certain way to be taken seriously in the dating world or at work. For me, modest dressing is tied to my faith.

"When I started wearing the hijab in high school, we only had black or ivory ones in these terrible fabrics that we got from Muslim conventions once a year or from overseas. Or we would wear neck scarves from fast fashion stores as hijabs, which aren't meant to be worn on the head or to be washed as often as you have to wash a hijab. I started going to thrift stores and buying silk scarves and wearing those as hijabs. So when I showed up to school, my classmates were like, *Oh my god!* Like I had gotten a new haircut or something."

> **"We're really focused on making sure we have every hijab a woman needs in her wardrobe, whether she's working out in the morning or getting married."** — Melanie Elturk

DESIGNING FOR EVERY OCCASION

"In 2010, my husband, Ahmed Zedan, and I began a modest fashion clothing line, Haute Hijab. Quickly, we saw that 70 percent of our revenue was actually coming from hijabs. Our customers are really thirsty for hijabs. I would travel across the U.S. and even into Canada looking for vintage scarves. I would buy thousands at a time. We would wash them in our bathtub. Then we'd photograph them in our apartment and post them for sale online every week. I was definitely drawn to the classic prints: chain links, anything animal print, the really beautiful Hermès- and Chanel-style of prints.

"We have a luxury line, which has hand-embroidery, beautiful laces, and Swarovski crystals. We're really focused on making sure we have every hijab a woman needs in her wardrobe, whether she's working out in the morning or getting married. You spend so much time, effort, and money on your look, so it only makes sense that you spend the same amount on making sure that your hijab looks just as beautiful."

Melanie Elturk is the CEO of Haute Hijab.

TRADITIONAL TOPPERS

Much like the hijab, these five traditional headwear pieces have special meanings and purposes—they serve as more than just an accessory.

TURBAN

Most popularly worn by the Sikhs, the turban is worn to represent their faith. It is meant to signify equality and honor among all those in the community.

RASTACAP

The rastacap is a round crocheted hat worn by those who follow the Rastafari religion, largely based in Jamaica. The caps often incorporate the Rastafarian colors: red, yellow, and green.

HEADDRESS

The headdress is a sacred garment given to select members of the Indigenous community in a ceremony. There are many different styles of headdress, depending on one's tribe. Today, headdresses are most often worn only for traditional ceremonies.

AYAM

The *ayam* is a traditional Korean winter cap mainly worn by women. It is often adorned with luxurious embroidery, tassels, and even crystals.

KUFI

The kufi is a short, brimless, rounded cap that is often worn by Muslim men during prayer. It is also a traditional hat popularly worn by men in West Africa.

FASHIONING MODESTY

Leah Vernon has more than just really good style. She is a Muslim fashion influencer, a model, and the author of *Unashamed: Musings of a Fat, Black Muslim*. Through fashion, Vernon uses her creativity and personal style to redefine the idea of what modest style can be—particularly showcasing how it can work for both plus-size girls and girls of all races. Here, Vernon shares a few of her most captivating (and entirely fabulous) outfits.

"For my birthday shoot, I basically frolicked around the city in this very hot and loud ensemble. People kept stopping me and asking if I was a celebrity. 'Almost,' I told them."

Photographer: Eric Puschak

Photographer:
Maryam Saad

WHAT DOES MODEST STYLE MEAN TO YOU?

"It means choice. I've been told so many times that I'm not Muslim enough, or not Muslim at all, because I don't fit into [the popular perception] of what modesty is. At some point, I had to learn what modesty meant for me. For some, modesty is wearing all black, and for others, it's a short-sleeve shirt. To me, it means a choice of how much (or how little) fabric you want to wear."

HOW WOULD YOU DESCRIBE YOUR STYLE?

"Bodacious. Loud. A conversation starter. A palate cleanser."

HOW IS MODEST FASHION REPRESENTED IN THE MAINSTREAM FASHION INDUSTRY?

"Modest fashion is a booming trend represented in stores and on the runway. It has surpassed just being a Muslim thing. Now it's for whoever wants to do it. Which is awesome. But, with the commercialization of modest fashion, there are still many voices and bodies that are left out. Like mine, for instance. I am a fat, Black Muslim girl. I never get to see myself represented in the modest fashion movement. Oftentimes, white-adjacent, thin, and pastel-wearing Hijabis and Muslim girls are championed [in the media] over everyone else. What about the "other" Muslim girls? The alternative ones. The ones with tattoos, and the ones who don't wear traditional hijabs. The ones who are fat, short, or dark-skinned. Where's our representation?"

"I've worn [the hijab] for a long time. Now, I mostly wear my hijab in the style of a turban. It's been up and down, and down and up. Right now, it's my crown."

"I designed this entire outfit and got it custom made for my birthday. Leo season was in full effect."

Photographer: Maryam Saad

Photographer:
Moon Reflections
Photography

"I enjoy taking different eras and making them my own. I felt like a Roaring '20s gal during these shots. I have a lot of shoots that I love, but the passion and intensity in my eyes are what gets me in this one."

"I felt like I had truly made it when I was flown down for this shoot in Mexico, even though my bank account was at zero."

Photographer:
Alexis Devaney

HIJABS ON THE RUNWAY

Hijabs are increasingly popping up on the runway and in major fashion campaigns. Brands such as Fendi, Burberry, Max Mara, and more have incorporated hijabs into recent luxury collections shown at fashion weeks.

Fendi

Burberry

Max Mara

Somali-American model **Halima Aden** is the first Muslim, hijab-wearing supermodel to take over the fashion world.

Aden has paved the way for Muslim models and made history along the way: she became the first model to wear a hijab while gracing the covers of several magazines, including *Teen Vogue*, *British Vogue*, and *Allure*, and in campaigns for brands such as American Eagle and Fenty Beauty (among others).

Halima Aden on the runway for Christian Cowan

She's also walked the runways for major brands including Max Mara, Dolce & Gabbana, and Alberta Ferretti. In 2020, however, Aden announced that she would be quitting the runway, saying that she often felt pressured at fashion shows to wear her hijab in ways that compromised her beliefs.

Below, explore Aden's rise to fame through the years.

1997: Aden was born in Kakuma, a refugee camp in Kenya, after her family fled the civil war in Somalia. A few years later, she and her family moved to the U.S., settling in Minnesota.

2016: Aden competed in the Miss Minnesota USA pageant and became the first hijab-wearing contestant in the history of the pageant to win.

2017: Aden quickly caught the attention of model agents and was signed to IMG Models.

2018: She became an official UNICEF ambassador and continues to raise awareness for refugees in her home country.

2019: Aden became the first Muslim model to wear a hijab and burkini in the *Sports Illustrated* swimsuit issue.

2019: She collaborated with the brand Modanisa on a collection of headpieces, including headscarves, hijabs, and turbans.

BURKINIS VS. BIKINIS: WHY NOT BOTH?

Speaking of modest dressing! A burkini and a bikini may seem like two drastically different garments. But they each come with similar scrutiny—and an opportunity for empowerment.

BURKINIS

A burkini is a modest form of swimwear that covers the entire body except the face. When Halima Aden became the first model to wear one (with a hijab) on the cover of *Sports Illustrated's* swimsuit issue, she faced criticism. She later said, "Some people are not going to like me . . . My whole motto is 'Don't change yourself, change the game.' And that's exactly what I'm trying to do."

BIKINIS

Women wearing bikinis have repeatedly been scrutinized and objectified, too, though in a different way. In some contexts, bikinis are viewed as too sexy and *not modest enough*. Still, many women today continue to rock bikinis for events such as pageants, claiming that how they dress shouldn't influence how others perceive them.

ENTERING THE ARENA

Muslim women are incorporating their hijabs into the world of sports. Major athletic brands are innovating on the headwear as a result. Brands such as Nike and teams such as the Toronto Raptors have begun selling performance hijabs.

But it's not just major labels. Meet two emerging brands, Olloum and TudungPeople, that specialize in creating sportswear hijabs, all of which are ready for the court while proving that modest style can apply to all sorts of arenas.

TudungPeople

TudungPeople

Olloum

TudungPeople

Olloum

TudungPeople

STANDING TALL

By rocking high heels, men and nonbinary people are walking tall, using footwear to push the boundaries of gender expression for themselves and the queer (LGBTQ+) community.

WHEN DID MEN START WEARING HEELS?

Today, high heels are largely considered a women's shoe, but did you know this footwear was first worn by men? The origin of heels dates as far back as the 10th century, but they became most prominent around the 16th century, with roots in Asian and Persian cavalries. Soldiers were documented wearing heels while riding horseback, as the shoes helped their feet stay in the stirrups (a reason why many of today's riding shoes, including riding boots and cowboy boots, still have heels).

Red carpet star Billy Porter.

LIFT OFF

High heels helped designers **Henry Bae** and
Shaobo Han walk away from childhood shame.

Henry Bae and **Shaobo Han** are the cofounders of **Syro.**

"The staring never stops. With my head held high and heels click-clacking, I don't [care] about what other people think."
— Shaobo Han

SHARING HISTORY

The two co-designers of Syro, a men's heel brand in New York City, are both part of the LGBTQ+ community. They share a similar background that inspired them to launch their brand. They both grew up with an appreciation for "feminine" fashion, and often felt a sense of shame whenever they wanted to wear these kinds of pieces. "We both grew up sneaking into our mothers' closets, trying on their dresses, jewelry, and of course high heels," says Bae. "We knew we were breaking an unspoken rule about gender and couldn't yet comprehend the weight of these norms." Han agrees, adding of his experience, "It was shameful. I knew I was doing something forbidden."

FINDING PRIDE

It wasn't until their later years, when Han and Bae finally began finding high heels in larger men's sizes, that they realized their draw toward femininity was actually very common, and that something as simple as wearing women's shoes could greatly express how they felt on the inside. "The moment I first wore heels, fit for my large adult feet, was heaven-sent," says Bae. "Everything felt right. It was humorous, and amusing, but also powerfully natural." Han says wearing heels and starting Syro have greatly informed his own gender journey as a result. "It took so much work to unlearn the shame I had around my femininity," he says.

UPLIFTING SPIRITS

With Syro, the two founders hope to create heels for men (and women!) that ignite a sense of confidence and positivity—for both themselves and their customers. "Syro came out of our own selfish desire to wear heels," says Han. "We just wanted cute shoes that would fit in with our everyday wardrobe, and we had a hunch that we weren't the only ones." Bae adds that they want to create a heel style that fits every comfort level—from first-time heel wearers to major stiletto lovers. "Our mission is to offer and celebrate variety," he says. "Some want their heels to shatter [gender norms] with every loud step of their six-inch platform heels, while some want to tiptoe into their femininity with an understated style that keeps a low profile on the streets."

CREATING AWARENESS

Bae and Han also hope to use their brand to create visibility for the LGBTQ+ community. "There's still so much to fight for," says Bae. "Queer people are getting fired, jailed, and murdered all around the world. For us, wearing heels is an empowering, public display of queerness. We're not afraid. We feel entitled to our safety, and we demand the right to express ourselves."

THE HISTORY OF MEN'S HEELS

History shows that men in heels is not a new concept.

Roker's men's heels

HOW DID MEN'S HEELS BECOME POPULAR?

In the 17th century, heels became popular with Europe's upper class, where the footwear was embraced by both men and women. The most famous adopter of the shoe was King Louis XIV of France, who ruled the European country for 72 years. The royal particularly favored heels, which may have had something to do with his height (he was 5 feet, 4 inches). In fact, during his reign, the king even implemented a law stating that only members of his court were allowed to wear his signature red heels, which served as a symbol of political privilege and status. (This signature color, cementing the wearer as wealthy or powerful, isn't far off from today's designer heels—Christian Louboutin's expensive stilettos, for instance, all have a recognizable red bottom, too!)

HOW HAVE MEN'S HEELS EVOLVED OVER TIME?

In the 18th century, men's heels began to fall out of fashion: men deemed them too impractical and effeminate. Still, as the years carried on, the shoes began to make a comeback on men—though in more subtle ways. In the 19th century, tall riding boots with heels were worn with pantaloon pants, and cowboys wore ankle boots with heels to ride. In the 1960s, dandies, including The Beatles, began rocking sleeker versions of heels, such as lace-up dress shoes. In the 1970s, disco platforms for men even became a trend, with singer Elton John regularly wearing them on stage. In the 1990s, the band Kiss rarely performed without their staggering platform boots, either. Flash-forward to today, and men on Hollywood red carpets are reclaiming heels, too.

HEELS IN POP CULTURE

These famous celebrities have rocked heels and made them mainstream.

Prince

Lil Nas X

Cody Fern

TRAILBLAZER: BILLY PORTER

Billy Porter is one of Hollywood's most exciting stars to watch on the red carpet. He first rose to fame after starring in the musical *Kinky Boots* on Broadway: his Tony Award–winning performance was all about encouraging the audience to accept individuality, look out for one another, and allow people to simply be themselves.

THE SHOE MUST GO ON

Porter's exciting sense of style on the red carpet is all about continuing on this idea—pushing boundaries and serving up new ideas, much like his *Kinky Boots* character did. There is no garment too bold or over-the-top for him to pull off, and one recurring piece that he incorporates into his looks is heels!

"I grew up loving fashion, but there was a limit to the ways in which I could express myself. When you're Black and you're gay, one's masculinity is in question. I dealt with a lot of homophobia in relation to my clothing choices. I was silent for a long time. I was trying to fit in with what other people felt I should look like. When I landed a role in *Kinky Boots*, the experience really grounded me in a way that was so unexpected. Putting on those heels made me feel the most masculine I've ever felt in my life. It was empowering to let that part of myself free." — Billy Porter

DESIGNING CHANGE

Alim Latif's journey from scientist to shoemaker fulfilled his larger destiny.

HOW I STARTED DESIGNING MEN'S HEELS

"I wanted to create a brand that is more inclusive and accessible. I trained to be a scientist and studied biochemistry at university. I have always been inquisitive, and while science satisfied that side of me, I always wanted to do something technical and creative. I trained to be a shoemaker and took up designing shoes for my brand, Roker."

CHANGING PUBLIC PERCEPTION

"When you say *heels*, people tend to imagine a stiletto heel. But viewpoints are changing. Cuban or stacked heels (about two to three inches tall) are growing in popularity and are not particularly seen as something feminine. My heels challenge the idea of masculinity versus femininity. I've never been interested in a thin stiletto heel as a practical functional item: they are very delicate, and I can't imagine them going with a size 45 (U.S. size 12) men's shoe. When working in heels, and in particular men's heels, form and function are so important."

HOW SHOES CAN MAKE A DIFFERENCE

"We are now seeing people challenge the concept of masculinity. What does it mean to be a man? Heels have always been worn by men throughout history and were seen as something very masculine, but as society changed, so did this idea. Heels can be very empowering. Women often say they feel empowered by heels, so why can't this apply to others? Working with the LGBTQ+ community has made me understand how important footwear can be, and how difficult it can be to get the footwear you want. It's important to have the right to choose what you want to wear."

Alim Latif is the founder of Roker. He is based in London.

A BEGINNER'S GUIDE TO WALKING IN HEELS

1. START WITH A LOWER HEEL HEIGHT.

Go higher as you get more comfortable.

2. MAKE SURE THE OVERALL FIT OF THE SHOE IS RIGHT, TOO.

Too narrow or too big can make learning to walk in heels that much more difficult.

3. EVENLY DISTRIBUTE YOUR WEIGHT ON YOUR FEET WITH EACH STEP.

A common mistake is putting too much weight on the toe or heel. No wobbling allowed!

5. DON'T FORGET TO WALK WITH CONFIDENCE!

Strut down the street with your head held high.

4. TAKE A SLOWER PACE.

Walking in heels is a marathon, not a sprint. (You simply won't get places as quickly as you would in sneakers.)

MIGHTY
MAKEUP

Makeup can be used as a tool for creativity. But it's not only about getting glam: beauty junkies are channeling their cultures into their looks, using their faces as a canvas for self-expression and pride.

THE POWER OF MAKEUP

Makeup is often thought to "improve" one's personal appearance, but today it is being used as a tool to enhance—not improve!—one's own natural beauty. Makeup artists are using their craft as a way to embrace their own sense of style, and finding striking ways to celebrate their own cultures' distinctive approaches to beauty.

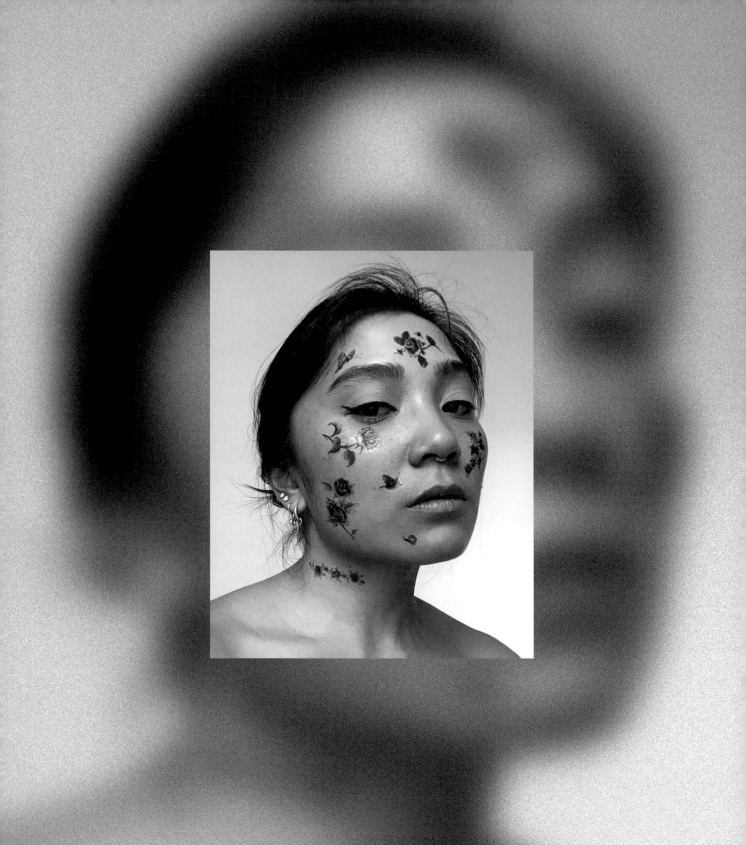

Justine Carreon is an editor at *Elle*.

THE BEAUTY OF ME

Growing up, a lack of representation made **Justine Carreon** question her own beauty, but she has grown to realize that her culture and roots are what make her special. Now she's using makeup as a tool for creativity and self-confidence.

FINDING MY SPACE

"Beauty ideals in Asia differ wildly from Western ideals. I am Filipino-American, so I straddle two worlds of clashing beauty standards. Growing up I struggled with trying to appeal to both. It doubled my self-consciousness as a teenager. The fact that I didn't fulfill these limited standards of beauty reinforced the false notion that what I looked like was never pretty enough. My image wasn't reflected back on television or in magazines, so understandably I wanted to look 'more white' and 'less Asian.' That meant I had awful skunk-streak highlights that didn't mirror the celebrities I admired, like Britney Spears, and forced myself to wear foundation four shades too light for me in high school because the shade for my complexion wasn't found in department stores."

REALIZING MY WORTH

"Lighter skin is favored in Asia, but I am naturally very tan. I was frequently discouraged from spending time in the sun. 'You're so dark' was a 'harmless' comment thrown my way by relatives on a regular basis. It's a common criticism in Filipino communities. It's a dangerous attitude and affects me personally to this day—a family member recently sent me papaya soap to help lighten my skin. Instead of using it like I did as a child, I threw it away. I had to reconcile with the fact that beauty is multifaceted and does include women like me. Opposite to what I believed growing up, there is not a single archetype of what beautiful looks like. This shift is partially due to both media and brands including women who look more like me and other marginalized people. This is why representation matters—so impressionable young girls and boys can see themselves reflected in popular culture and not feel like an outsider in society."

SEEKING OUT MY SHADE

"Finding my foundation shade is so rare that as soon as I find a brand that makes it, I am a loyal customer. Even when I have professional makeup artists custom mix shades for me, the chances of them understanding my complexion is a toss-up. Approaching color is different with my skin tone, so you can't apply the same game plan that you would on someone with fair skin. Thanks to brands like Fenty, we're seeing more inclusive business models that offer wide shade selections. It's a godsend—I'm glad that the next generation will never have the same experiences I had growing up not seeing myself reflected in media and in the makeup aisle. We can all finally participate, even in this limited scope, and hopefully society will continue to grow."

WHAT WORKS FOR ME

"A curling iron is no match for my stubbornly straight Asian hair, but my friends' hair will curl with ease. For everyone who enjoys makeup, skincare, or hair, it's a personal journey in figuring out your own formula, and you play as you go. That's the beauty of, well, beauty: experimenting and having an outlet to express yourself."

HONORING HENNA

Halima Hossinzehi uses henna to express her culture and proudly demonstrate her heritage. It gives her the opportunity to embrace an ancient art while letting her imagination run wild.

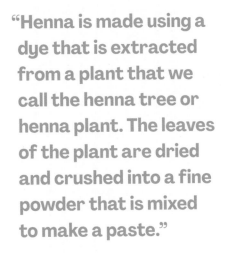

"Henna is made using a dye that is extracted from a plant that we call the henna tree or henna plant. The leaves of the plant are dried and crushed into a fine powder that is mixed to make a paste."

Hossinzehi's striking henna was done by her sister-in law Saba Jangizi, a professional artist.

Halima Hossinzehi is a Baloch-Canadian student in Southern Ontario.

"Many people use henna for hair dye as well: I have used it on my skin, nails, and hair. When used on its own without any additional ingredients, henna typically takes about an hour to dry. It stays for around two weeks before it starts to fade."

"Henna art signifies celebrations such as weddings, a birth of a child, birthdays, graduations, and religious ceremonies. I've been getting it done since I was very young—I would say two or three years old! It's completely safe."

GLAM SESSION

Nyma Tang is a prominent beauty influencer with her own successful YouTube channel. In her videos, she focuses particularly on Black beauty brands and reviews foundation shades for darker complexions—creating a much-needed space in an industry that's known to be exclusionary.

FINDING MY AUDIENCE

"I launched my YouTube channel because I was frustrated over the lack of inclusivity in the beauty industry. I also realized that I could make a difference in people's lives. When you think of beauty, you think about makeup, but some people don't feel comfortable with the lack of inclusivity that they see. I would say the Black beauty community is definitely a very, very, very supportive community. We need more resources and pull, and our value needs to be taken more seriously outside of just complexion. We have more to offer than just talking about and making sure there is enough makeup for all complexions—although that is such a big concern and desire for us to fix. I think we have more value than what the beauty industry tries to place on us in this moment."

MY MAKEUP EXPERIENCE

"It definitely was difficult to find my shade. Before I started my series, I could name on one hand the foundations that were accessible to me and that I could make work. But they can't deny us anymore. Our voice is too loud. Now, there are 15 to 20 foundations that I can use. There's definitely been progress, but it's still hard. To this day I have to go to six different stores to find the foundation shade I need. That's something that I'm hoping will change. And I definitely think the formulations of darker foundations need to change. What differentiates Black-owned brands from non-Black-owned brands is their perspective on pigmentation, undertone colors, and their understanding in creating products."

FIGHTING FOR INCLUSIVITY

"The feedback and the reaction I get is the most important part of the job that I do—impacting people's lives in a way that they feel seen and heard, and also feel like they have some sort of representation. Helping them learn to accept and love their skin tone is one of the most satisfying things about this job."

SHADES FOR ALL

Until recently, beauty brands have failed to offer foundation shades for every skin color. But that's all changing. Makeup is becoming more inclusive and offering more variety to reflect all customers.

THE POWER OF YOUTUBE

These three beauty vloggers are using their channels to foster a community where all are welcome.

CELEBRATING BLACK BEAUTY

Jackie Aina is one of the most-viewed Black YouTubers on the platform. Like Nyma Tang, she provides a space where Black makeup lovers can get information on the latest foundations, makeup, skincare, and more.

TACKLING ACNE TOGETHER

On her channel, **Elaine Mokk** posts candid videos about her ongoing struggle with acne. She provides a space where fellow acne sufferers can share and relate. She also posts makeup reviews and provides helpful tips for those who wish to conceal their acne, though one shouldn't be ashamed!

EMBRACING MEN'S MAKEUP

Ivan Lam's YouTube channel showcases a variety of makeup looks that he encourages all men, women, and nonbinary makeup lovers to try out. He is one of many prominent men on YouTube who are redefining how—and by whom—makeup can be used.

MY FACE IS MY CANVAS

Jennifer Bear Medicine is an Indigenous makeup artist based on the Blackfeet Indian Reservation in Browning, Montana. She uses her eyelids as a canvas to celebrate her traditional Apsaalooke culture.

"I choose things like artwork, beadwork, appliqué designs, and even tattoos that catch my eye."
— Jennifer Bear Medicine

HOW DID YOU GET STARTED WITH MAKEUP?

"I fell in love with makeup when I was 19 years old.
I started out trying to recreate looks that I liked, and
I discovered that I *could* do it. So I just kept practicing
by looking at pictures and recreating them. I've always
had a steady hand, so once I felt I was good at makeup
I decided to start drawing pictures on my eyelids."

WHERE DO YOU DRAW INSPIRATION
FOR YOUR LOOKS?

"I look for photos that catch my attention. Then
I check the details to make sure that I can recreate
it and that I have the colors I'll need. Sometimes I get
an idea I want to try, such as the issue of Missing and
Murdered Indigenous Women and Girls. Then, I'll look

for specific photos. I do these looks, especially the
tiny pictures, on myself. I haven't tried doing them on
anybody else yet. I feel like they wouldn't look as good
because I'm so used to drawing in a mirror."

YOUR WORK CELEBRATES YOUR CULTURE—WHY IS
BEAUTY A POWERFUL MEDIUM TO DO SO?

"I didn't grow up around my culture. The looks I do, prais-
ing others who are expressing their cultures through
dance and everything else I'd like to be involved in, makes
up for me missing out on my own culture. Makeup is a
good way to express my culture because I'm good at it.
I still have so much to learn, but makeup lets me celebrate
what I feel was lost."

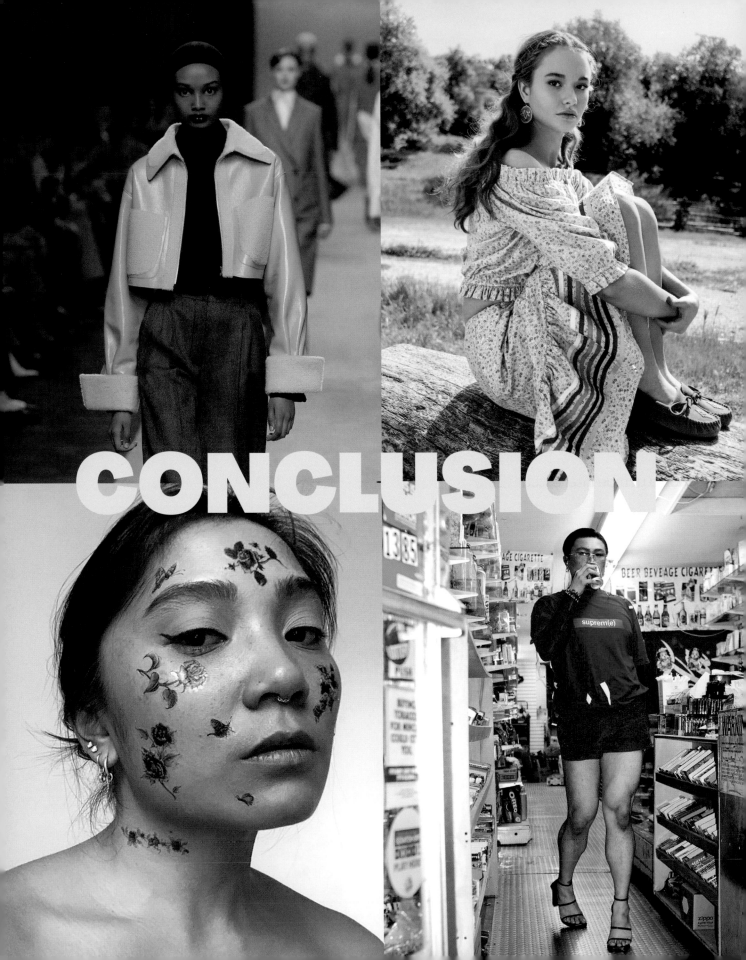

CONCLUSION

Now that you've had a chance to explore—and hopefully become inspired by!—all the different ways fashion and beauty are being used to empower people and celebrate their cultures, I ask you one key question. Where do we go from here? Style clearly has the ability to convey a message that goes beyond just the aesthetics. It can express individuality, defy stereotypes, and tell stories about ourselves that ignite a larger conversation. So, how will you use style to express *your* story?

We're at a time when cultural pride and activism are more important than ever, and should you be interested in all things style, it's an opportune moment to use what you wear for a larger purpose. This can mean embracing your culture's traditions in a way that makes sense for your personal style. This can mean not shying away from your natural body type, hair texture, or complexion, but rather finding ways to enhance and amplify it. It can mean wearing that one piece in your wardrobe that you may have been too self-conscious or shy to wear. Whatever way you choose, owning who you are—and *embracing* it through how you present yourself—is a powerful way to put your own stamp on the world.

I hope the inspiring people in this book compel you to find pride in your own story. I know that this book is something I would have liked to read when I was a teen. While I am now infinitely proud of my Indigenous heritage, it is something I fully accepted and came to terms with later in life. Hearing the stories in this book would have inspired me to be more interested in, and proud of, my own culture. As humans, we all struggle with self-image; it is a common shared experience. But the new shared experience should also be lifting one another up and admiring others' unique perspectives.

Fashion and beauty are there to be discovered and played with—there is no expiry date for when you choose to do this. That is the beauty of it all. What you put on—whether it's heels, makeup, or a traditional garment—is entirely up to you, as is how and when you do it. Going forward, the only rule you should think about when dressing up in the morning is to have *fun* with it. Be unapologetically you. That is one trend that will never go out of style.

Miigwetch for reading,
Christian Allaire

ACKNOWLEDGMENTS

I would like to first and foremost thank my rock star editor, Mary Beth Leatherdale, as this book would have been completely impossible without you. Thank you for all of your thoughtful notes along the way (and for doubling as my therapist at times!). I'd like to thank everyone at Annick for believing in this book, especially Kaela Cadieux for your invaluable input. To all the subjects featured in this book, thank you for the endless inspiration. A big *miigwetch* to my parents, Nancy and Peter, and sister, Alysha, for the constant support. And to my friends, who always keep me going.

IMAGE CREDITS

COVER
Photo courtesy of Jamie Okuma/Cameron Linton

CONTENTS
Clockwise from top left:
Photo courtesy of Nyma Tang/Anthony Owusu
Photo courtesy of Kap/Laura Munley
Photo courtesy of Haute Hijab/Caleb & Gladys
Photo courtesy of Syro

INTRODUCTION
Clockwise from top left:
Photo courtesy of Jamie Okuma/Cameron Linton
Photo courtesy of Tranquil Ashes
Photo courtesy of Leah Vernon/Maryam Saad
Photo courtesy of Durrant Santeng/Nalin
Springer

SEWING TRADITION
P. 3: Sewing Tradition intro page
Photo courtesy of Jamie Okuma/Cameron Linton

PP. 4–7: My Culture's Couture
Photos courtesy of Christian Allaire

PP. 8–9: Winning Ribbons
Photos courtesy of Jamie Okuma/Cameron
Linton

PP. 10–11: Spiritual Connections
Photos courtesy of Anita Fields
Osage blanket: National Cowboy and Western
Heritage Museum
Headshot: Melissa Lukenbaugh
Illustrations by Jacqueline Li

PP. 12–13: Paving the Way
Photos courtesy of Bethany Yellowtail

P. 14 : #Trending
Clockwise from top left:
Photos: Courtesy of Geronimo Louie, Lauren
Good Day, Doneese Bull-Buffalo

P. 15 : #Trending
Clockwise from top left:
Photos: Courtesy of Stephane Richard, Geronimo
Louie, Maile Hampton, Alyssia Sutherland

MY HAIR, MY WAY
P. 17: My Hair, My Way intro page
Photo courtesy of Durrant Santeng/Nalin
Springer

PP. 18–20: Love Thy Locks
Photos courtesy of Modupe Oloruntoba/Andy
Reeves/Uyapo Ketogetswe

P. 21: Over the Rainbow
Photos: Courtesy of Quanah Style

P. 22: At Any Length
Photo courtesy of Chelene Knight/Katherine
Holland

P. 23: Natural Hair on the Red Carpet
Clockwise from top left:
Photo of SZA by Kevin Tachman/Getty Images
for *Vogue*
Photo of Janelle Monae by Steve Granitz/Wire-
Image
Photo of Zendaya by Dimitrios Kambouris/Getty
Images

P. 24: Growing Freedom
Photos: Courtesy of Haatepah Clearbear/Hadar
Pitchon

P. 25: Growing Freedom
Photo courtesy of Phillip Bread

PP. 26–27: Growing Freedom
Photos: Courtesy of James Jones

P. 28: The Art of Braids
Photos courtesy of Durrant Santeng/Nalin
Springer

P. 29: Braid Styles
Illustrations by Jacqueline Li

LEVEL-UP
P. 31: Level-Up intro page
Photo courtesy of Surely Shirley/David Love
Photography

P. 32: Why We Cosplay
Photos courtesy of Kap/Laura Munley

P. 33 Why We Cosplay
Photo courtesy of Tranquil Ashes/THE SLEEPY
MUSE

P. 34: Why We Cosplay
Photo courtesy of Casey Nichole/Maro Louden
Photography

P. 35: Why We Cosplay
Photo courtesy of Surely Shirley/Danielle Joy
Studios

PP. 36–37 My Body, My Choice
Photos courtesy of Kap/Laura Munley

PP. 38–39: Breaking the Status Quo
Photos courtesy of Surely Shirley/ Danielle Joy
Studios/Danielle DeNicola

PP. 40–41: Crossing Boundaries
Photos: Tranquil Ashes/Cookie Monsta/Leslie
Jones

P. 42: DIY IT!
Photo: Casey Nichole/Argonian Photography

P. 43: Cosplay Tools
Illustrations by Jacqueline Li

HEAD STRONG
P. 45: Head Strong intro page
Photos: Courtesy of Haute Hijab/Caleb & Gladys

PP. 46–48: Taking Control
Photos: Courtesy of Haute Hijab/Caleb & Gladys/
Salwa Marzouk

P. 49: Traditional Toppers
Illustrations by Jacqueline Li

PP. 50–53: Fashioning Modesty
Photos: Courtesy of Leah Vernon/Eric Puschak/
Maryam Saad/Alexis Devaney/Moon Reflections
Photography

P. 54: Hijabs on the Runway
Photos: Courtesy of Fendi, Burberry, Max Mara

P. 55: Halima Aden sidebar
Photo courtesy of Christian Cowan

PP. 56–57: Entering the Arena
Photos: Courtesy of TudungPeople/WUSVUS
Productions and Olloum

STANDING TALL
P. 59: Standing Tall intro page
Photo: Santiago Felipe

PP. 60–63: Lift Off
Photos: Courtesy of Syro

P. 64: The History of Men's Heels
Photos: Courtesy of Roker

P. 65: Heels in Pop Culture
Clockwise from top right:
Photo of Prince by Kevin Mazur/WireImage for
NPG Records 2011
Photo of Cody Fern by Axelle/Bauer-Griffin/
FilmMagic
Photo of Lil Nas X by Dimitrios Kambouris/Getty
Images

PP. 66–67: Trailblazer: Billy Porter
Photos: Santiago Felipe/Matthew Murphy

PP. 68–70: Designing Change
Photos: Courtesy of Roker

P. 71: A Beginner's Guide to Walking in Heels
Illustrations by Jacqueline Li

MIGHTY MAKEUP
P. 73: Mighty Makeup intro page
Photo courtesy of Jennifer Bear Medicine

P. 74: The Beauty of Me
Photo: Courtesy of Justine Carreon

PP. 76–77: Honoring Henna
Photos: Courtesy of Halima Hossinzehi

PP. 78–80: Glam Session
Photos: Courtesy of Nyma Tang/Anthony Owusu

P. 81: Shades for All
Illustrations by Jacqueline Li

PP. 82–85: My Face Is My Canvas
Photos: Courtesy of Jennifer Bear Medicine

CONCLUSION
Clockwise from top left:
Photo courtesy of Fendi
Photo courtesy of Bethany Yellowtail
Photo courtesy of Syro
Photo courtesy of Justine Carreon

BACK COVER
From left to right:
Photo courtesy of Haute Hijab/Caleb & Gladys
Photo courtesy of Syro
Photo courtesy of Tranquil Ashes/Cookie
Monsta